FEARLESS Soul|Shots

31-Day Devotional

Soul|Scripting + More

Tiffane Gayle

A SimplyTChic! Soul|Full Experience

Fearless Soul|Shots
31-Day Devotional + Soul|Scripting

ISBN 979-8-218-14720-4

To fear: Thank you for showing up so I could meet the courage and discipline living inside me.

To everyone who has walked with me on this beautiful journey called life. And to those who have inspired me to face fear through their words and actions.

Contents

Preface

What are you transmitting to those nearest and dearest to you—fear or courage? That is, when you encounter opportunities or challenges, is your usual reaction one of fear or of courage? Would you like to develop the skills needed to consistently overcome fear with courage? Those are questions I wrestled with for years as I let fear cause me to settle for less than I knew I could achieve. From as far back as I can remember, I have witnessed people I love live with paralyzing fear instead of taking up their God-given space in this world. Oftentimes, when we don't know what to do, we feel scared, choose fear instead of courage, and do nothing.

I learned from experience that this struggle to choose courage instead of fear is an all-too- common form of spiritual attack. For instance, one day I was speaking with a friend and as we updated each other on life's victories and challenges, she shared that she felt like her family was under attack. She asked whether I felt the same regarding some of the issues my family was facing at the time. My answer to her was, *"Yes, girl! The Bible tells us that there is enmity between us and the devil so we beefin' for life! The enemy of our souls would love for us to believe his lies, throw in the towel, and quit before our brilliance can be uncovered, shared, and shining brightly. But he can't stop us from being great unless we let him! Our mission should be to take up the shield of faith and extinguish the fiery darts of the enemy, uncover our brilliance, and share it with the world!"*

As a woman and mother, I was discouraged as I saw women—including myself—living with fear, and when I saw fear paralyzing my own children, I was enraged! I saw clearly the liar and thief that is fear. I was simultaneously intrigued because I learned through my own experience and the experience of others that fear seems to be a map to our soul; therefore, saying yes to fear can enable us to live soul|fully. In other words, fear can either stop us from moving through the process of overcoming, or it can stir up the courage that is sitting inside us waiting to be accessed and bring us closer to our soul|calling.

Our collective pain and inaction got my attention, angered me, and caused me to grieve. But our collective brilliance and awaiting soul|full legacy motivated me to change—to act on my own fears and encourage others to do the same. *Fearless Soul|Shots* is one result of my commitment to action. My lived experiences coupled with those of family members and other soul|sisters caused me to see that saying yes to fear was the only way to answer the calling of the soul! As you journey through *Fearless Soul|Shots*, you will learn to use seven "shots" to help you overcome fear, engage courage, and uncover your God-given brilliance—one SHOT and one devotional at a time!

My hope is that *Fearless Soul|Shots* will help you say yes to fear and answer your soul's calling and allow your brilliance to shine like never before. I believe it will help you quiet that persistent, pesky voice that says you are not capable of living a life of brilliance. It will shush the voice that says your gifts are nonexistent, too small, or insignificant. It will set fire to the voice that says your life is not worth living, that your pain is impossible to heal, or that you aren't disciplined enough to see anything through. Following the truths in this book will still the inner voice that says you are incapable of change.

This book uses a unique style for drawing your attention to the importance of concepts related to the soul. On the cover and throughout, you will notice that I used a vertical bar (|) instead of the horizontal bar (-) to create the compound "soul" words (e.g., soul|full, soul|friend, soul|care). The use of the vertical bar is intentional because perspective is everything. God is the creator of our souls; therefore, it is impossible to live a soul|full life without looking to our creator! Nonetheless, many of us focus primarily on horizontal relationships and circumstances. Although horizontal relationships are important and horizontal circumstances are real, we should not allow the horizontal view to dictate and distract us from the vertical (God) view.

Cultivating your vertical relationship doesn't mean that you will live a life devoid of problems; it means that the Lord will be your anchor and that he will sustain you through every trial. Focusing first on your vertical relationship only strengthens your horizontal relationships and your ability to navigate the difficulties that life presents. Using the vertical bar throughout this devotional is a way of reminding you and me to look up because that's where our help comes from. You need the Lord's help to operate with power, love, and a sound mind. When you feel you've had too many losses and want to give up, you need God's help to receive clear vision and to live with courage and discipline. To make legacy decisions and live soul|fully, you will need help from the Lord. The vertical relationship between you and God is your most valuable relationship. It should be your main focus, and it should inform how you respond to your horizontal circumstances and relationships. The vertical brings understanding and depth to the horizontal; it gives right perspective to every aspect of life.

It is my prayer that choosing courage will become a movement—a movement that starts with you choosing courage, discipline, and healing. There are but two choices: fear or courage. It's time to choose—time to start your transformation. This devotional will help you choose courage and implement discipline so you can live with a soul|full perspective as you radiate your God-given brilliance. Being ready to start and choosing courage aren't feelings; they're decisions to face fear and heal in spite of your feelings. This decision will cause you to live strong, bold, courageous, and contagious. Both fear and courage affect our legacy, and both are transmissible. What do you want to spread or infect those you love with—fear or courage? What do you want your legacy to be? Let's journey through this devotional and together choose courage and discipline as we answer the call of our souls. Remember that your strength comes from the Lord.

I look up to the mountains; does my strength come from mountains? No, my strength comes from GOD, who made heaven, and earth, and mountains.
Psalm 121:1–2

Introduction

Through my own experiences and those of others, I have had a front-row seat to the reality that fear can either stop us from moving through the process to the other side, or it can stir up the courage that is sitting inside each of us waiting to be accessed and thereby bring us closer to our soul|calling. Many times we start the process of facing fear and healing but stop when the pain gets too deep or when we don't know the answers or when we doubt our God-given brilliance. We are afraid to heal because in order to heal, we must reveal and feel the pain of traumatic experiences all over again. What we don't realize is that we are already feeling the pain and the fear whether we do so intentionally or not. Fear oozes out in so many ways and, unfortunately, on so many people.

In my case, my kids were becoming paralyzed partly because I was unknowingly oozing fear on them by not exercising courage when I was faced with fear! If we are unable to identify fear in ourselves, it is likely that if we take an intentional look at those closest to us, we will see it in them. If we are paralyzed with fear but don't see it in ourselves, most assuredly someone around us does. Fear has a way of limiting us: There are places we aren't willing to go both mentally and physically because of pain and fear. There are people who are essential to our soul|calling that we can't engage at a deeper level because of pain and fear! Fear stops us from arriving at previously scheduled God-appointments because our hands, tongues, hearts, and souls are tied and we're unable to move. I'm here to assure you that if you choose to stop running from fear and run straight toward it, you will arrive—only you can make the choice. Choosing courage puts us in a position of future wisdom and informs the way we speak and share with others on the journey. It allows not only our courage and brilliance to be unleashed, but it also unleashes the courage and brilliance of those we were created to serve!

It's unfortunate that our minds often focus more on our challenges than our victories! But that shouldn't surprise us because our adversary is mission-minded! He is serving up lies, hoping that doubt and confusion will paralyze us, lull us to sleep, and cause our brilliance to be dimmed thereby rendering us ineffective. Thank God we get to choose who and what we listen to and what we set our minds to. I'm choosing to listen to God and set my mind to faith, courage, discipline, and love. I choose to shine, learn, forgive, and win. I am training my soul to focus on soul|full living!

Soul|friend, we are not of those who shrink back! Under pressure, grapes, olives, and carbon can produce something beautiful. We too have the power to transform into something magnificent when pressed! The view from the mountaintop is definitely higher and breathtakingly beautiful, but it is the climb that builds strength, character, and perseverance. Our story and our climb can inspire others to keep going when they find themselves in the valley. The challenges we face are simply an invitation to make a choice: evolve or remain the same.

Choosing to evolve means that growth will occur, and another layer of our God-given brilliance will be uncovered. Your choice to evolve no matter how uncomfortable it may be is critical because when you evolve, many of your people will evolve too. I choose to live with the growth and discomfort that come with facing fear and activating courage rather than living with a false sense of comfort that fear provides. In the midst of every storm, I seek courage, joy, love, wisdom, revelation, and peace, and those are realities that find me! During the storms of life, God either delivers me out of the storm or uses the storm to clear and illuminate my path. Along the way, I ride the waves seeking and celebrating victories (because they too are all around us) even in the face of fear and adversity!

Soul|friend, your God-given brilliance is calling. It is why you are here, what makes you unique, and what enables you to live soul|fully! Until you say yes to your brilliance and to fear, you will always be unfilled. Embracing your brilliance brings glory to God, serves others, and satisfies you. You were created to serve; indeed, serving is your legacy! There are people who need your distinctive life experiences and gifts to be delivered as only you deliver them! I encourage you to serve fear notice by behaving like you serve an unlimited, fully present God and to choose faith, courage, and grit each time fear hands you an invitation. You were made to shine brilliantly, and if you don't quit, you will win. Your brilliant, soul|full life is waiting for you. It's time to start calling the SHOTS(SS)!

I have not arrived, but I am evolving one SHOT and courageous decision at a time. I invite your soul (mind, will, emotions) to evolve with mine.

If you wait for perfect conditions, you will never get anything done.
—Ecclesiastes 11:4 TLB

Saying Yes To Fear

Some years ago, I wrote the poem, "My Name Is Fear," for my daughters and to share with members of my community, or so I told myself. The truth is the dialogue had been going on in my mind and spirit for some time, and it still does. When something has a hold on you, if you don't break it, it will slowly break you! The spirit of fear—oh, it doesn't come to play—it comes to stay for generations! It comes on assignment to try to discredit the plan of God in your life and to steal your legacy.

In time, I discovered that the real reason I wrote this poem was driven by the hope that whoever heard or read it would have the audacity to choose courage in the face of fear. What I know for sure is that if you don't choose courage, fear will choose and rule you. You have the God-given authority to bind and loose. So, I encourage you to bind fear and loose courage, power, love, and a sound mind. If we allow it, fear can be a gift that unleashes our God-given brilliance and leads us to live with soul|sourced courage!

Read "My Name Is Fear" and consider what fear has stolen from you. Are you waiting for all of the conditions to be right before you step out? Have the fangs of fear been gnawing at the necks of those you love? Fear is contagious, but so is courage—spread that! I invite you to make a soul|decision partnered with action so that fear can lead you to courage. The truth is I wrote this poem for my daughters; I wrote it for you, soul|friend; and I wrote it for me too.

> My Name is Fear
> My name is Fear, I am a thief—I rob you before you even begin.
> I whisper in your ear as if I were your friend.
> I don't think you will succeed—so just come over here and chill with me.
> See isn't that much more comfortable? I mean, who likes being out of their comfort
> zone?
>
> My name is Fear, I am a thief—I rob you of your dreams.
> I stand on the stage of your life, and I sing.
> You can do it too . . . never just wave this white flag of surrender and dream . . .
> dream about what you could do—yeah, yeah, that's it.

See all those dreams, they're just counterfeit.
Other people can do it, but no, no, not you—you just sit down awhile with me and be
    Cool.

My name is Fear, I am a thief— I will have you living the same year over and over and
    over and call it your life.
I torment you in the brightness of daylight—then say, that's just the way life is.
I attack your self-esteem and have you torture yourself with regret of missed
    opportunity.
I make you settle for less . . . yeah, that's it—I make you waste your brilliance.

My name is Fear, I am a thief—I will have you—Wait, what? What did you just say?
    Did I ask you your name?
God calls you his beloved, says you were chosen from the beginning, and he didn't
    give you a spirit of fear but of power, love, and a sound mind.
You no longer believe my lies? He told you to be bold and courageous, so you're
    going to stand on your stage and sing; fear no longer dictates your destiny.

Instead of running from your fears, you're going to follow them because they're the
    GPS to your soul?
Say what! You're out of control! Let me move on to the next soul; you've
    become much, much too bold!

—Tiffane Gayle

Moving from Fear to Brilliance

Some people think of a "shot" and envision something administered by a nurse in a doctor's office. That type of shot may be used to treat or prevent disease. Others might think of and swear by their nutrient-dense juice or wheatgrass shot for its energy boost, amino acids, minerals, vitamins, and antioxidants. I personally enjoy a great juice flight! Still, others might imagine a glass filled with spirits, which is typically consumed in one swallow. The more of these shots a person ingests and the faster they ingest them, the stronger the effects.

These shots have been known to leave people inebriated, incapacitated, and wishing they had never indulged but keenly aware that their soul is searching for more. The truth is their search will only be satisfied by seeking and cultivating a relationship with God as they face fear so they can uncover and live from their God-given brilliance.

I have a different take on the term shots—what I call Soul|SHOTS(SS). These SHOTS(SS) are about inviting God into every aspect of your life so you can become who you were created to be. If you don't come to know the brilliance of you, not only will you not recognize and misuse your brilliance, but you will allow others to do so as well. Connecting to God's presence, transforming your soul, confronting fear, and exercising discipline are great ways to start practicing soul|care. Soul|care requires acknowledgment, choice, courage, and endurance, and it will stretch you in ways that sometimes feel like you're at a breaking point. But soul|care will ultimately awaken you to your God-given brilliance. That brilliance is your unique shine, through which you come to understand and embrace your gifts, talents, and limitations. The awesome thing about your limitations is knowing that where you are weak, God is strong. Thus, part of soul|care is learning to acknowledge your weaknesses, so God's strength can rise up in you. Soul|care enables you to embrace where you are and all that you are created to be!

God was intentional when he created you; you owe it to him, to the world, and to yourself to live your life with intention by saying yes to his will and way. The SHOTS(SS) described in this book are not intended to be used as a ritual but as a response to God's love and goodness and to the brilliance he has placed in you. To live in the fullness of God's intent, we must engage in soul|care and say yes to courage. I can testify that the SHOTS(SS) described on the following pages are proving to be a roadmap of sorts to my soul; they guide me in creating intimacy with God and intentionality in my daily living. I am confident that they can be valuable to you as well.

What are SHOTS(SS)?

You can think of SHOTS(SS) as a prescription (RX) to be taken daily or as needed to get the best results. Soul|SHOTS(SS) consist of seven life skills that have proven to help a person flourish:

S Silence. Practice silence so you can hear God. (Psalm 46:10)

H Honor. Honor God with thanksgiving. (1 Thessalonians 5:18)

O Opportunity. Focus on God-opportunities vs obstacles. (Exodus 4:2)

T Thoughts. Your imagination is powerful; you win there, first! (Philippians 4:8)

S Speak. Speak life to yourself and others! (Proverbs 18:21)

S Script. Write it down; make it plain! (Habakkuk 2:2–3)

S Strengthen. Move and nourish your soul and your body! (3 John 2)

SHOTS(SS) are a critical part of the process of evolution; we will explore each of the SHOTS(SS) in the next section of this book. For now, I want to introduce the concept and share some of the benefits. First, SHOTS(SS) help me live with daily discipline, which I have found to be an integral part of becoming. In order to grow and overcome fear, you must learn to love discipline. Okay, maybe not love discipline but acknowledge the importance it plays in your transformation and be a willing participant in living a disciplined life. I liken the SHOTS(SS) to archery. If you plan to hit the intended target, you have to slow down, remove distractions, build strength, balance, focus, aim, and keep practicing. You will not always do every step perfectly and hit the intended target every time, but don't let that stop you. Keep aiming, shooting, and adjusting. Imperfect action is better than standing still and living with regret! Engaging with Soul|SHOTS(SS) allows God's arrows of love, peace, wisdom, courage, direction, influence, and so much more to permeate and awaken your soul as you surrender to his will.

Soul|SHOTS(SS) can be life-changing, intimate, and orchestrated by God if you allow them to be. The SHOTS(SS) are taken behind the scenes—part of your daily practice—when no one is watching, and they will have a major impact on your ability to live soul|fully and allow God to guide you in building your legacy. These SHOTS(SS) lead you back to the assignments that God originally imagined and designed for you. They illuminate your soul's purpose, penetrate you, and open you up to your God-given brilliance—the highest version of you!

But you must do the work by showing up for your soul! I pray that you allow these SHOTS(SS) to infuse and open your soul to everything you were created to be, everything you already are. May you have the audacity to be a fearless SHOT-caller and remember to always follow your soul; it knows the way.

Setting Yourself Up to Win

Setting yourself up to win anything begins in your mind with the choice to start! As the Scripture says, "Do not despise these small beginnings, for the LORD rejoices to see the work begin" (Zechariah 4:10 NLT). You can be your worst opponent or your best proponent—you choose. If the voice you hear the most is yours, it should be cheering you on and speaking life to your soul. One way I set myself up to win is by committing to say yes to fear (by exercising courage) and discipline. When I have to make a decision and I am feeling tempted to say no because of fear or laziness (let me call it what it is, at least for me), I pray and deliver an immediate yes! My yes means that I act out of courage and God's strength, not my weakness. It challenges me to behave like I believe God's Word is true, knowing that with him, I can handle whatever challenges come my way. My yes to fear enables me to see and act on God-opportunities and build trust in my creator and the ability he's placed in me. It also leads me toward my soul's calling. My yes (your yes) is an inspiration to others even if they never say a word.

There was a time when I was not a good friend to my soul. My soul desired to spend more time with God, face fear, nurture and share my gifts, strengthen my relationships, eat healthier, and work out consistently. But after so many half-hearted, failed attempts at making these life changes, I became chronically disappointed with myself because I knew that I wasn't living with the discipline, courage, and consistency I was capable of. Can you relate? Ugh, there is nothing like being disappointed with yourself! I know the feeling well—I felt it when I looked in the mirror, and I heard it when I talked to others, especially my husband and children. Finally, I accepted that I had a choice to either take full responsibility for my actions and my soul|talk or keep living below the standard I desired for myself.

That's when I started practicing what you are about to read in this devotional, and it has helped me to live with greater discipline and intentionality in my relationships with God, others, and myself. As a result, I am closer to God and proud of the woman, wife, mother, daughter, and soul|friend I am becoming. Being courageous enough to take up your God-given space in this world and celebratory of the person looking back at you in the mirror as you answer the call of your soul is truly a gift . . . it is freedom!

A key to setting myself up to win with this devotional experience was committing to begin each day with SHOTS(SS) and/or a devotional. I believe that creating that habit has opened the way for my personal transformation over time. That frustrating first hour of the day that some of us spend hitting the snooze button or scrolling social media can turn into a power hour with the SHOTS(SS). You can redeem the time and add strength to your soul and discipline to your day. It can be a reminder of who and whose you are and empower you to speak to and direct your day instead of having your day speak to and direct you.

Together, the Soul|SHOTS(SS) and daily devotionals will rouse your soul and spark an unrelenting desire in you to live out what God has placed in you. Although early morning may not be your favorite time of day, it is time over which we typically have the most control, so we can choose to use it to our benefit. Setting aside time each morning to engage with the SHOTS(SS) and/or a devotional is one way to be intentional and schedule your priorities. It increases your chances of spending time with God and inviting him to help you direct and design your days, weeks, months, and inevitably your life. Ultimately, do what works for you, but for me, taking SHOTS(SS) first thing in the morning has worked really well.

The SHOTS(SS) are soul|care and provide a daily navigation framework. They add value and should be practiced from this day forward; this is not a one-and-done approach to life transformation. They can be practiced alone or in tandem with the daily devotionals that follow. Either way, the SHOTS(SS) help you get closer to the creator of your soul and live a more disciplined life. I know I keep mentioning discipline—that's because it has become a game-changer for me.

Living a life without discipline in any area (i.e., spiritual, financial, relational, or health) will cause you to live below your calling, leave you unfulfilled, and diminish your legacy. Living a disciplined life will cause you to feel proud of yourself, break generational cycles, and create a legacy that future generations will be proud to emulate. The places and people God is calling you to require a level of discipline that can't be faked. Living with discipline is a challenge and depending on your perspective, it can appear to be about restrictions. In truth, a disciplined life is a life full of rewards and freedom.

For example, exercising discipline to wake up early to practice the SHOTS(SS) can positively affect the direction of your day as well as your mindset, words, actions, impact, and overall lifestyle. Living with discipline in spending and saving can give you the freedom you desire in retirement, allow you to take vacations with no financial regrets, and bring freedom in everyday giving and living . When you are working toward a goal, discipline not only helps you reach your goal but it also increases your level of trust and respect for yourself and builds character along the way. Exercising discipline in your relationships will build trust, intimacy, and joy. I've seen discipline help people break addictions such as overeating, alcohol and drug abuse, and the need for pornography. A student, who exercises discipline in studying and time management can enjoy peace, good grades, and freedom that come from living a disciplined life. Remember it isn't freedom if it costs you your peace, sobriety, integrity, or character. Discipline is a game-changer, and it takes discipline to practice the SHOTS(SS) or accomplish anything worthwhile, for that matter.

Engaging with the SHOTS(SS) and the Devotionals

The seven Soul|SHOTS(SS) unveiled in this section are designed to help you jump-start your soul|transformation. The description for each SHOT begins with a Scripture that captures the deeper meaning of that SHOT followed by brief reflections on how you can practice that SHOT to further the transformation you desire. Each SHOT concludes with a list of ways you can intentionally choose to face fear and choose courage—one day at a time.

    The SHOTS(SS) can and should be practiced the way God leads you, so your practice times will vary. Do what you can, not what you can't! For example, one week you may choose to focus only on one SHOT for the entire week. Another week, you may choose to engage with two SHOTS(SS) daily and then dive into the devotional; another week you may take one-minute SHOTS(SS) each day, and other days you may make space for all seven. When you get off track (because we all do), don't beat yourself up and stay off track! Acknowledge where you are, how you got there, make some adjustments, and move forward—whatever you do, don't quit! You could even ask a friend to go through this devotional journal with you as a form of connection and accountability. Listen to your soul; give it what it needs.

    Whatever you do, soul|friend, remember that this is your space, and soul|care is between you and God. You are God's gift (meant to be opened and given willingly) to humanity, and that gift came with extraordinary soul|assignments (i.e., people or areas of service). Completion of those assignments is possible through you because of God's hand in and on you. Your methods or audience might change, but your soul|assignments remain the same. You are assigned and equipped to pour the gift of you onto others, live with your soul full, and leave a legacy of soul|full living! The SHOTS(SS) help you regulate, create, and dominate. Take the SHOTS(SS) and set yourself up to evolve and win. Never underestimate the power of your God or your soul— start by calling the SHOTS(SS)!

Shot 1 – Silence

"Be still, and know that I am God!"
Psalm 46:10 NLT

What is the first thing you do when you are really trying to hear something? You get quiet and close, right? If you're anything like me, you might even shush the people around you. That's because the closer and quieter you get, the louder you hear. Sitting still and practicing silence can definitely be a challenge. It's something my soul simultaneously struggles with and desires. Therefore, I am intentional in saying, "Practice silence!"

Carve out time to practice being still. With all the noise around you—both solicited and unsolicited, it's hard to distinguish whose voice you're listening to and certainly hard to hear God speak. When we get quiet and pray for God's will to be done, we open our souls to hear God's gentle whispers. Wisdom and revelation often manifest during quiet time spent alone with God.

Create an environment to connect with your soul. Whether your stillness includes reading your Bible and meditating, sipping tea, praying, or lying still in your bed when you awaken each morning or go to bed each night, make time to be still and recognize who God is. This SHOT challenges you to remember and acknowledge who's on your side. Be still and let him do what neither you nor any level of busyness, money, accolades, sex, shopping, social media likes, food, alcohol, titles, religion, drugs, or lies can do! Be still and know that he alone is God and gives wisdom to those who ask.

Application
1. Pray, breathe deeply, and invite God in—ask for wisdom and revelation.
2. Ask God if there's anything he's trying to deposit in or disconnect from you.
3. Sit quietly and wait for the Lord.

Be still and know

silence →

Shot 2 – Honor

"In every thing give thanks: for this is the will of God in Christ Jesus concerning you."
1 Thessalonians 5:18 KJV

Great is his faithfulness—that is the reason we are here. Arriving at this point in life means you've overcome something. That makes you an overcomer. God deserves our reverence simply for who he is. Regardless of the challenges or blessings in your life, honor God with thanksgiving. Gratitude is one of the most important things we can reflect on each day. It is one of the most important things we can offer in all of our relationships. Thank God for his love, wisdom, favor, provision, mercy, and grace. Invite God to be your guest of honor each day as you reflect on his goodness. And don't forget to honor the people God has called you to do life with.

Application
1. Offer a prayer or song of thanksgiving.
2. Listen to worship music.
3. Make a list of things and people for which you are grateful.
4. Send handwritten notes and text messages or call loved ones.
5. Consider how your blessings and trials have developed character and perseverance in you.

Give thanks, always

honor

Shot 3 – Opportunities

"Then the LORD asked him, 'What is that in your hand? 'A shepherd's staff,' Moses replied."
Exodus 4:2 NLT

Oftentimes, faith feels risky, but you can't have faith and control at the same time! A soul|sourced, faith-risk can be the difference between living soul|fully and living with fear and regret. Sometimes, we focus more on the obstacles in front of us than the opportunities. Many "obstacles" are simply opportunities for our brilliance to shine. I double dare you to start looking for opportunities, in particular the God-opportunities all around you. Take every opportunity God gives you. If you look, you will see them. Sometimes, we are so focused on what (resources and talents) we believe we don't have that we forget to put some respect and use on the resources and gifts we do have.

What's in your hands? Take inventory and put a demand on it. Trust God. Act with courage, and when you fall, get up with new knowledge, make adjustments, and move forward in faith! Falling is part of the process—it creates space for growth and is part of your testimony. Don't be afraid to fall; rather be afraid to stay down or never try. You are surrounded each day with opportunities to break generational cycles, make faith-moves, form new habits, and face fears. Keep your eyes, soul, and heart open to God-opportunities!

Application
1. Ask God to help you discern and act on every God-opportunity.
2. Seek opportunities to serve, love, give, create, and practice courage.
3. Remind yourself that regardless of how unready you feel, your current location is the perfect place to start learning and evolving.

Seek
Act
Create

opportunities →

Shot 4 – Thoughts

"Summing it all up, friends, I'd say you'll do best by filling your minds and meditating on things true, noble, reputable, authentic, compelling, gracious—the best, not the worst; the beautiful, not the ugly; things to praise, not things to curse."
Philippians 4:8

Living soul|fully requires that you guard your thoughts. We have thousands and thousands of thoughts each day that go unsupervised. You are the gatekeeper of your mind, and many of your issues can be traced back to an unchecked thought. Check your thoughts. Life has a way of distracting us from dreaming. You need to set aside time for soul|dreaming, which is imperative for soul|care. Our minds were created to think thoughts that power our souls. Therefore, winning or losing always begins in your mind. It's impossible to win if you don't play or aren't on your own team.

Speaking of teams . . . if your team isn't inspiring your thoughts and actions toward your brilliance, it's time for a team meeting and possibly some team cuts. Connect to the Mind Transformer and allow him and his Word to transform your thoughts and mind. Meditate on the best possible outcome, not the worst. Seek God's vision for your life, then begin to visualize and move toward soul|full living in every area of life. Allow your imagination to travel not just to your future but to the future of those your soul was created to influence.

Application
1. Ask God to cause your thoughts to align with his will.
2. Visualize and see yourself taking steps to manifest vision in specific areas.
3. Visualize potential challenges and see yourself overcoming them, so when challenges arise, you will be thinking about overcoming, not about being overcome.
4. See yourself celebrating your victories and the victories of others.

Protect
Dream

Thoughts

Shot 5 – Speak

"Words kill, words give life; they're either poison or fruit—you choose."
Proverbs 18:21

We have the privilege and power to choose our words. What does your God-talk, soul|talk, and others-talk sound like? Don't talk crazy to or about God's creation—and that includes you! You have the ability to speak things into existence. Choose to speak soul|filling, gift-stirring words to yourself and others. Speak life to your soul and into every situation, recognizing that your words have power.

Application
1. Speak things that are not yet (in this realm) as they are in the spiritual realm to shift your thoughts and surroundings so that you can pull things from the spiritual realm into the earthly realm. As you do so, there will be a shift in your perspective and therefore the mood of a place (e.g., home, work, school) or situation (e.g., relationships, finances, health).
2. Affirm God's Word with daily confessions regarding your purpose, health, family, and other aspects of your life.
3. Record your confessions and listen to them when needed for reinforcement.
4. Speak words that edify others.

Life
love
Legacy

Shot 6 – Script

"And then God answered: 'Write this. Write what you see. Write it out in big block letters so that it can be read on the run. This vision-message is a witness pointing to what's coming. It aches for the coming—it can hardly wait! And it doesn't lie. If it seems slow in coming, wait. It's on its way. It will come right on time.'"
Habakkuk 2:2–3

Writing down your God-given goals, dreams, vision, and soul|assignments is essential soul|work. The very act of writing (i.e., scripting) helps you make your vision plain; it brings clarity, gives direction, and provides hope. And when scripting is paired with action, it can lead to the victory for which your soul was created. Writing can be a cathartic process, allowing you to sift through your feelings. This is an important step in the transformation journey because our feelings often indicate areas in which we need to invite the Holy Spirit to minister and uncover truth.

Application

1. Write and pray over your vision (e.g., personal development, marriage, parenting, finances, retirement) and goals. Do scheduled check-ins to help you keep your vision top of mind.
2. Keep a journal next to your bed as oftentimes in the quiet of the morning, God speaks and inevitably if you don't write down what he says, you will forget.
3. Record God's faithfulness, your self-reflections, and recollections of special moments with those you love.
4. Use your journal or notes on your phone to set three to five specific intentions for each day.
5. Soul|script as you engage with your SHOTS(SS).

Writing brings clarity + direction

Shot 7 – Strengthen

"Dear friend, I hope all is well with you and that you are as healthy in body as you are strong in spirit."
3 John 2 NLT

It is crucial for both your soul and body (physical and mental) to prosper. You've only got one of each, so as you fuel your soul, be sure to fuel your body too. This includes what you consume (through your eyes, ears, and mouth), the way you move, and how you snooze! Two components of legacy are mindset and lifestyle. Pass along a legacy of a healthy soul and body to your loved ones. Too many times we put off taking care of our mental or physical health until it is in a state of malfunctioning. Create and commit to a preventative plan that serves your soul and your temple. The plan should include tapping into the Strength-giver through worship and prayer; proper rest; healthy eating; exercise (physical and mental); and seeing a medical doctor, dentist, and therapist as needed.

Application
1. Before excuses or life can get in the way, take your SHOTS(SS), commune with God, walk, stretch, and/or do a cardio workout upon rising each morning.
2. Commit to keeping your mind challenged and your body hydrated and well nourished. Rest when needed.
3. If you get off schedule, embrace grace and refuse to let a missed day turn into a missed week.
4. Invite family and friends to join in and practice nourishing your souls, moving your bodies, exercising your minds, scheduling appointments, and eating well.

Soul

+Body

strengthen

23

31 Days of Devotionals

Living with your soul full requires you to say yes to fear and embrace your soul|assignments. Remember, we are not waiting for conditions to be perfect but for a yes from God and from our soul, regardless of the conditions. You can start each day with premeditated fearlessness by choosing to focus on the truth of who God is and, therefore, who you are. The daily devotionals give you a guideline to speak God's Word and to propel yourself into action—even in the face of fear.

This section presents a 31-day devotional designed to be read and experienced over and over as you evolve. The devotionals will help you snatch back what is yours: courage, peace, joy, legacy, and the power of seeing with your soul. Your God-given soul|assignments are God's investment in you. I believe that his investment extends beyond you and factors in all the people and places he's called your soul to serve. Do everything in your power to give him a good return on his investment by choosing to live from your soul. Storm your fears by activating courage while living with discipline as you pour out your brilliance on the world. May you lean into fearless soul|full living, run with it, and pass the baton to others because your part in the race is not the end.

At various points, the devotionals are punctuated with a thought-provoking quote and question selected specifically for our journey. I encourage you to reflect on each quote and question as you work your way through the devotionals. I find questions and quotes to be a source of motivation and inspiration; they help me to go deeper and become more of who I was created to be. A well-phrased question helps me seek to understand, clarify, and unlock the potential of my soul. Questions and quotes have greatly influenced me as a woman, wife, mother, daughter, and friend; essentially, they have helped me evolve. As you work through the devotionals, you'll likely adopt favorite quotes and questions—ones that deeply resonate with you and your journey. Feel free to flip to a question or quote that is especially meaningful to you and meditate on it as the Spirit leads.

Each devotional draws on a passage of Scripture, which is then incorporated into a brief discussion followed by a confession. Each devotional ends with an opportunity for you to practice soul|scripting as a means of encouraging you to think deeper about how the Scripture pertains to your life.
Praying and meditating on Scripture will help align your desires with what God intended for your life when he created you. As you spend more time in his Word, you will become more familiar with his voice and gain courage and clarity regarding the direction you should go. May his favor and your courage take you to the places your soul dreams of.

I pray that you choose to show up for the life you've been granted and that your soul always says yes to his will and way! I will be cheering you on and believing that it is well with your soul as you progress through the devotionals.

Let the first quote be your invitation to engage with this devotional and your life!

For. His. Glory.

Quote

Show up for the expected
and the unexpected!

Nona Ferguson

Question

Why is it important for you to
show up
and how are you choosing to
show up
at this time in your life?

Day 1 - Transformation is Necessary

Don't copy the behavior and customs of this world, but let God transform you into a new person by changing the way you think. Then you will learn to know God's will for you, which is good and pleasing and perfect.
—Romans 12:2 NLT

Transformation starts in your mind. It is vitally important to get the imprint of others off us and to get the imprint of God on us by renewing our minds. Don't waste your life, gifts, or brilliance trying to be who others are or who they are telling you to be. That's not how you were designed. Can't nobody **be** you—like you! You can only meet your soul's calling as deeply as you've met your soul's creator. So don't follow culture; follow your Creator. You were constructed and born an original MASTERpiece (literally a piece of the Master), so don't try to be a duplicate of someone here on earth. Living a life that does not embrace who you were created to be is the true imposter syndrome.

How has the world (i.e., family, friends, school, career, religion, or social media) programmed you to think about your life, purpose, distinctions, relationships, finances, or health? It's time to refine your mind and align your thoughts to God's Word, so your plans can be established and succeed. Invite the architect of your soul to transform you. He aimed you at greatness before you were in your mother's womb. The God version of you is the highest (most brilliant) version of you; it brings glory to God, serves others, and gives you a deep-seated sense of joy, peace, and contentment.

Changing the way you think doesn't happen by accident. Change is a continual choice and is informed by your input. You cannot afford to start your day or live your life on autopilot. You may not be able to change every situation, but you can start by choosing what you think about. Don't let your mind be a playground for unproductive or negative thoughts; let God transform your mind.

Confession

I choose to allow God and his Word to transform my mind and shape my thoughts as I discover his good, pleasing, and perfect will for my life!

SoulScript

_____

_____

_____

_____

_____

_____

_____

_____

_____

_____

Write down some tangible ways to begin transforming your mind and
changing the way you think.

Day 2 - The Command Means Your'e Capable

Have I not commanded you? Be strong and courageous. Do not be afraid; do not be discouraged, for the LORD your God will be with you wherever you go.
—Joshua 1:9 NIV

If you have parents, younger siblings, nieces, nephews, or children, it is highly likely that you've heard or said, "Didn't I tell you . . .?" Well, that is what I hear God saying in love to us in Joshua 1:9. In other words, God is asking, "Didn't I already tell you to be strong and courageous. Don't be scared; I got you. And I am going to be with you wherever you go. So let's get to it!" I believe that the word *be* is a demand on what God has already placed in you. Be strong and courageous —it's in you. God only commands what you have the ability to produce.

"Have you stopped doubting yourself yet?" he asked me. I remember when I felt my soul calling me to homeschool my youngest two daughters. It felt scary, so naturally, I ignored the calling. I was working a contracted position and was pleased with the flexibility, pay, and work. I was like, *"God, you are looking at two (my husband and me) amazing public school graduates. Why would we homeschool? Also, Lord, in case you forgot, we have four children's college tuitions to consider, so I will keep dropping these blessings off at school and get this paper!"* I promptly landed two more contracted positions: one for an organization doing work on the educational achievement gap, and another with the public school system. As I completed those contracts, much was revealed and confirmed to me, so I decided to circle back to the last instruction my soul had given me. (Sidenote: Always follow the last instruction God has given you. Alas, I am learning to listen the first time, but I don't always get that right!)

Anyway, one contract was ending in eighteen months and after talking with my husband, I chose not to renew the other contract. We withdrew our youngest two children from the school they were attending and spent our days in the summer sun creating a plan for the coming school year. My colleagues and some family members thought I had lost it. And at least once every other day, I agreed with them! My mom couldn't figure out why I would spend the time and money to go to college only to eventually stay home with my children. I started getting calls from a "concerned" family member asking what the girls were learning each day. It was awful because I was often already doubting myself and wondering the same thing! Every morning, I asked God to help me not mess up my daughters' lives and make them stupid (as if that were possible; he had already created them to be amazing—just as he has created you and me). I also often wondered what college would accept them as homeschool graduates.

I started off being afraid that I would look bad and be blamed for every failure. Later, I realized that ultimately this wasn't even about me or my success; it was about my obedience and my daughters' future. Then I flipped the script on that fear and began looking for opportunities to exercise courage instead of focusing on obstacles. I started each day with a simple prayer and confession: *"God, be with us, and today I choose courage."* I cultivated space for strong family connectedness, character building, curiosity, independent learning, and passionate exploration. I also felt led to include fiscal responsibility in a way that hadn't been done before in our family. We laid out the vision, set goals, then worked backward.

Some days are breathtakingly beautiful, and some are really hard as we haven't completed the journey yet. At times I feel like an epic failure; other times, I feel as if I am on top of the world. But how I feel doesn't always match reality.

Now, ten years later and with only two years left on this journey, our 16-year-old is doing extremely well. She has earned 22 college credits and is taking all her courses at a local college. Our 18-year-old just graduated from high school with an associate of arts degree; she is a member of the college honor society and has her own digital marketing business. She was offered enrollment and renewable academic merit scholarships at every university she applied to. She's accepted a sizable academic scholarship to a private university with junior status and will be eligible to graduate with her bachelor's degree debt-free in two years!

Not only that, but my girls are also loving, compassionate, and responsible young ladies who know how to advocate for themselves and others. God was with us every step of the way. Blew. My. Mind. He told me to be strong and courageous because he was with me and not just with me but with my daughters also. And he will be with you too.

He commanded of me something I was fully capable of even though I struggle with math and structure. Ha! To God be the glory! His power was made strong in our weakness. Never doubt what God has placed in you, what he commands of you, and what you believe your soul is calling you to. When I shared this news with my cousin who is like a big brother, after his heartfelt congratulations, he asked, "Have you stopped doubting yourself yet?" The truth is, I still doubt myself and my ability sometimes, but what I refuse to do is doubt the God in me. His super on my natural is a brilliant combination!

Confession

I am strong and courageous because God is with me wherever I go!

_____

_____

_____

_____

_____

_____

_____

_____

_____

_____

Take a moment, close your eyes, and think about a challenging situation you are facing. Open your eyes and write about that situation as if it is victoriously behind you. Imagine the best possible outcome! Note how God was with you every step of the way.

Quote

Being fearless is an ongoing choice to practice courage. Courage doesn't manifest unless fear is present. Don't run from fear *run to courage!*

Question

When is the last time you placed yourself outside your comfort zone, and *what did you learn?*

Day 3 - Your Attention is Required

*Give your entire attention to what God is doing right now, and don't get worked up about
what may or may not happen tomorrow. God will help you deal with whatever hard
things come up when the time comes.*
—Matthew 6:34

When you feel yourself getting worked up (i.e., anxious, agitated, or fearful), remind yourself to take things as they come, not as you feel or fear. The same God who delivered you before—the same God who delivered victory to Esther, Deborah, Rahab, and a multitude of others—is working things out for you. Set your focus on today's victories. Bring tomorrow's concerns to God in prayer and praise.

Not long ago, I faced a challenging season in my life. I was fatigued, losing hair and weight, experiencing shortness of breath, finding unexplained bruises on my body, and having frequent migraines. I spent a lot of time seeing doctors. Through that process, a CT scan showed a nodule on my left lung, and I tested positive for an autoimmune disorder. I was scared.

We were praying, but my thoughts kept trying to override those prayers with fears of the worst possible outcome. The enemy of my soul was speaking in his native tongue (lie) continually. I had already lost two first cousins and a best friend—all at young ages and suddenly. Those losses fed my fear. I would think about the possibility of not seeing my daughters grow up, not growing old with my husband, and not seeing my own mother grow old. I was asking the Holy Spirit for direction. It seemed that answers from the health professionals were coming slowly or not at all. In spite of the negative thoughts, I began to set my mind to healing and giving God praise for all that I was grateful for. After many appointments and biannual checks, I learned that the nodule on my lung was consistent with a benign lesion—it wasn't growing; it wasn't cancer! After re-testing, the Mayo Clinic determined that the previous autoimmune test was a false positive result. Through the leading of the Holy Spirit, my research confirmed that my ferritin (iron stores) and hemoglobin were extremely low, and this had been exacerbated by another issue. When ferritin and hemoglobin are as low as mine was, people typically experience extreme fatigue, hair loss, debilitating migraines, and bruising! This can be cured with a blood transfusion or in some cases an iron supplement depending on the individual situation. Initially, I was so busy being worked up about death that I was not living. But unbeknownst to me, my symptoms were all because of low iron stores. Fear can cause us to focus on the wrong things, overestimate threats, and underestimate our God-given ability to navigate hard situations. Pay attention to and direct your thoughts to what God is doing at the moment, knowing that he will help you maneuver through hard things when they come.

Confession

Lord, I am attentive to what you are doing right now knowing that you will help me tread rough waters at the appropriate time.

SoulScript

What faith steps can you make now to remind yourself to take situations as they come, not as fear presents them?

Day 4 - Don't Forget to Factor in God

The LORD himself goes before you and will be with you; he will never leave you or forsake you. Do not be afraid; do not be discouraged.
—Deuteronomy 31:8 NIV

Once again our daughter's witty humor had me in stitches. She looked so beautiful on the FaceTime screen as she got ready for the first football game of the college season. I could see the excitement on her face as she talked about the two girls she had recently met on campus and invited to join her friends and her at the game. I was proud of all that she had accomplished that week. She had passed four nursing exams, introduced herself to new people, and was actively working toward becoming the woman God created her to be. I certainly loved seeing her radiant smile! As we got off the phone, she promised to send me a group picture later that evening.

When my phone rang two hours later and that beautiful face appeared on the screen, I was surprised and a little concerned—the game couldn't be over. When the voice I heard on the other end wasn't my daughter but her friend, I became even more concerned. When her friend put the phone to my daughter's mouth and gibberish came out, I was alarmed! Our baby girl (22 years young) had passed out at the football game. She was away at college—out of our physical reach but never out of God's reach! The ambulance was called, and she was transported to the hospital. The next call I received was the sound of my daughter crying. I had never been happier to hear her cry. But the words she spoke through her tears rattled my soul, "Mommy, it's worse than before; I can't move." The medical team got her hydrated and ran a series of tests. The next day, it was determined that she needed to wear a heart monitor and see a cardiologist.

At the time of this publication, we are in the middle of fighting the good fight of faith and looking forward to overwhelming victory in this situation! As we fight, our focus matters. As you fight, your focus matters. It's hard to fight if you're focused on losing. It's hard to fight if you aren't intentional about what you are thinking, seeing, and listening to. As fear attempts to silence and paralyze me, I am allowing God to settle my soul through his Word, the SHOTS(SS), and this devotional!

The Scripture above says that God goes before you; let's focus on that. In a relay race, the person who goes before you gets the best advantage that she can so that your team can be in the lead. God has gone ahead of you to give you the advantage. When Jesus ascended to heaven, he sent the Holy Spirit to comfort, guide, go before, and prepare the way so that you have the advantage. Not only is he with you as you go, but he also loves you so much and knows that along the way, you will doubt the possibility of what he promised. So, he says,

"I'm not going anywhere!" God has been, is, and always will be #teamyou! No matter what you're going through or who has left you in the past, you can count on God. Don't be afraid; don't believe the lies, and don't ever forget to factor in God! As we fight the good fight of faith with our words, prayer, music, and the Word of God, remember that the battle has already been won. Our heavenly Father has sealed the deal . . . we just have to believe and walk it out.

Confession

Lord, I thank you that you have prepared the way for me and have illuminated my path. I will not be discouraged, for you will never leave me. Because of you, I have the advantage, and I am counting it all joy.

SoulScript

What specific area do you need to focus on believing in faith that the Holy Spirit has gone before you (or a loved one) and cleared a victory path with your or their name on it? Write about it, thank God for making a way.

Quote

God's plan is for you to have an impact! You may impact millions or a select few. *Is either all right with you?*

Question

What person has had a
positive impact on your life?
Have you told him or her?

Day 5 - Love is Greater Than Fear

There is no fear in love. But perfect love drives out fear, because fear has to do with punishment. The one who fears is not made perfect in love.
—1 John 4:18 NIV

God is love; there is no fear in God. God's presence (love) drives out fear. The closer you are to God, the less power fear has over you. When you are feeling "fear-full," try more God through prayer, silence, worship, or Bible reading. Your input determines your output! Put more God in you, so more God will come out of you. As you spend time with God, you will get clearer on how to operate in your God-given brilliance, and that paralyzing fear will begin to decrease. When love/God created you in his image (where there is no fear), he created you with purpose and assignments. When you are operating in your purpose, his love in and for you will empower you to activate courage and fear less.

Confession

Lord, I thank you that you are perfect love and that you dwell inside me. Therefore, fear has no hold on me. I'm out here activating courage every chance I get!

SoulScript

_____

_____

_____

_____

_____

_____

_____

_____

Is there an area in your life that has been overtaken by fear or a situation that you are feeling fearful about? Write down some ways that you can activate courage and fill up on God. When we are God-full, we fear less!

Day 6 - Trust God

When I am afraid, I put my trust in you.
—Psalm 56:3 NIV

You are having a human experience on earth, so the spirit of fear will attempt to invade your thoughts and guide your actions. Some fears are seemingly insignificant. For example, what's the big deal if you are afraid to _____ (you fill in the blank)? But if you let fear dictate one area of life, the negative soul|chatter will chip away at you, and that fear will spread in you, mutate, and possibly spill over onto those you love. But when you feel afraid, you can trust and move in God. He cares about all the details of your life.

I tried to hide it, but I was embarrassed and tired of watching my husband and daughters enjoy the water on family vacations or on beautiful summer days, but I didn't have the freedom or courage to join them. For years I had carried my mother's, my grandmother's, and eventually my own fear of water. Sidenote: Don't go picking up and carrying other people's fears; you have enough of your own!

I made up my mind and learned to swim at the tender age of 46 in the middle of a Minnesota winter. I was fortunate to have had two amazing swim coaches for this learning experience. The pre-pool coach worked in tandem with the in-pool coach and taught about breathing, floating, and how the various swimming strokes move you through the water/life. I learned that when fear overtakes you in the water or in life, you will begin to drown.

One of the things that started off being a soul|irritant but ended up blessing me immensely was that we came together at one location for the pre-pool discussion but had to drive to another location for the in-pool lessons. The first few nights of driving in the dark and cold required a lot of soul|talk. I had to talk myself into saying yes all over again each time. Fear was telling me to go home, back to comfort. It was uncomfortable going back out into the cold, only to drive by my home, and persuade myself not to return to the comforts inside! It was uncomfortable jumping into a cold pool carrying the weight of fear. That pool really should have been warmer; I'm convinced that would have helped tremendously.

Although the conditions weren't ideal, I made up my mind to trust that God had directed me to this unique opportunity and that he would be with me every step of the way. I attended every lesson, jumped in the water immediately for bobs (before fear began speaking too loudly), and gave my full attention and participation. I used breathing techniques and soul|talk every step of the way. At the end of the first pre-pool session, the location of the in-pool experience was revealed. To my surprise, God in his infinite goodness, was bringing me out of my comfort zone and back to the very pool where I had been too afraid to learn to swim 34 years prior! He's so good. One of my confessions is that God would bring me back to every place where I have experienced a loss due to fear and allow me to experience a win! Swimming was always in me, but I needed to trust God, release fear, and embrace courage to get the win. Amazing swim coaches didn't hurt either!

Confession

The moment I sense the spirit of fear creeping up on me, I put my trust in your Word and your promises. My focus is on you.

SoulScript

_____

_____

_____

_____

_____

_____

_____

_____

Write something you're feeling fearful about and a short prayer regarding trusting God in this area. Thank him in advance for coming through for you. What step(s) can you make toward facing this fear?

Quote

Soul|full living is intentional. It is your choice
and your journey to become the
highest version of yourself ...
The version God imagined and created!

Question

What do you
imagine your soulfull legacy
to be?

Day 7 - The Gift of Your Surrender Is Peace

Don't worry about anything; instead, pray about everything; tell God your needs, and don't forget to thank him for his answers. If you do this, you will experience God's peace, which is far more wonderful than the human mind can understand. His peace will keep your thoughts and your hearts quiet and at rest as you trust in Christ Jesus.
—Philippians 4:6–7 TLB

Surrender it all to God through prayer and praise! What is your "**it**"? Surrender that thing to God. If your experience has been anything like mine, your "it" is likely going nowhere or getting worse in your hands anyway. So, let it go; give it to God, and every time that worry comes up say, "Lord, I give this to you, and I thank you for the answer!" See yourself worry-free in this area!

Surrender is not a sign of weakness but of strength. Strength begins with a decision to give your weakness to God. Being a mother has sent my potential for worry sky-high. And I had the nerve to think that it was going to get easier as they got older! Sometimes, I worry that we haven't given our children everything they need to survive in this world, but we have. We gave them Jesus, the Word of God, and our unconditional love. Additionally, we gave them opportunities and information while modeling respect, love, apologies when needed, forgiveness, lived-our faith, standards, integrity, character, boundaries, perseverance, and grit. Even though we have not and will not do everything right, we always come from a place of love and create an atmosphere for conversation. We have seen each of our daughters face fear and activate courage. Glory to God! Our best battles are fought on our knees and with our words. I know the transformation God has done in me, so I know he can do whatever is needed for anybody else. God sees exactly where our daughters are and where they need to be, and he knows how to get them there! The same is true for your situation. That is my peace. That is why I surrender. He has proven that his ways are better than my ways!

Confession

I bring everything to God in prayer with a heart of thanksgiving; then I enjoy the soul|rest that only comes from being in a relationship with him.

_____

_____

_____

_____

_____

_____

_____

_____

Write down your "it" in answer to the question in today's devotional. Then mentally practice seeing or imagining your "it" worked together for the good! Take a moment to consider and write down the top five things you are believing God for and write them out as a prayer. Be sure to take a praise break for the outcome you're expecting. Your hallelujah (highest praise) belongs to him not only for what is to come but for who he is and what he's already done!

Day 8 - Strong God

Fear not, for I am with you. Do not be dismayed. I am your God. I will strengthen you; I will help you; I will uphold you with my victorious right hand.
—Isaiah 41:10 TLB

No matter what your circumstance looks like or how you feel, God is with you. He strengthens, helps, and upholds you. So do not let the spirit of fear take hold of you. As believers, we have access to the inward strength of the Holy Spirit—we need this strength when difficulties arise. On our journey, we need God's strength to sustain us and help us to become, finish well, and shine brilliantly.

Receiving that call with bad news or walking into the hospital room of a terminally ill or deceased loved one—especially when it happens suddenly—is never easy no matter how many times you've done it. So many emotions flood your soul. In such circumstances, I have experienced overwhelming feelings of love, fear, pain, peace, confusion, and anger. Grief is a natural response to loss. To never grieve is to never have lost or loved. Like you, I have both loved and lost.

Grief doesn't give notice; it shows up unannounced! It appears in a smell, a memory, the thought of something you want to share, a dream, or a song. I miss the physical contact with loved ones that I have lost even though our love has transitioned into a spiritual connection. I feel their presence, courage, strength, peace, and love, and I take that with me wherever I go. Love and loving relationships are a gift. The love and good memories of those I've known and lost are what I choose to focus on. I allow those memories—the love, laughter, and even tears—to be a salve for my soul. I grieve with the hope that I will see my loved ones again and that in some way I can carry their legacies forward. I commemorate those closest to me that I've lost through storytelling, activities or events, and recipes. Each time I have lost someone, God has strengthened and upheld me even on the days when I thought I was too weak to go on.

Confession

Lord, in my weakness, you are strong. I will not fear. You are an ever-present help in my time of need. I am victorious through you.

Soul Script

_____

_____

_____

_____

_____

_____

_____

What are some ways that God has shown himself strong for you in the past? Take a moment to write down a few of the ways God has come through for you. Acknowledge that God has shown up before and that he will do it again. Share his goodness with a loved one and ask them how they believe God has shown up for them in the past.

Quote

Your proximity + pursuit of God determines what you believe, see, and hear as well as how you (re)act! God is your Commander in Chief; he gives the orders that lead to soul|full living! Don't ignore the gift of seeking God's kingdom, righteousness, and presence!

Question

How are you actively
seeking God's Kingdom
and his will?

Day 9 - God's Hand is on You

Because I, your GOD, have a firm grip on you and I'm not letting go. I'm telling you, "Don't panic. I'm right here to help you."
—Isaiah 41:13

Sometimes, situations arise due to our own decisions; other times, things happen because of decisions made by other people and are completely out of our control. Either way, situations can confront what we say we believe, make us panic, and doubt God and our calling. There was a man who chose to have an unloving firm grip on one of the people I love most in this world. But God's grip is stronger and never tires. She was far from home, but thankfully God and his hedge of protection are not confined to any four walls, and Psalm 91 is embedded deep in her soul. Under that pressure, she began to doubt who she was. Under that pressure, those who love her could have panicked, but we prayed and put pressure on the Word of God! That pressure produced something in her that she didn't even know was there: perseverance and strength. She began to speak life to herself, and she made some courageous decisions. In some situations, courageous decisions need to be made over and over. There is often a pull to go back to what you know. Keep saying yes to courage and yes to your brilliance even when the past is calling you back. Remember, God is here to help you.

There is a difference between man having a firm grip on you and God having a firm grip on you. God's grip is full of love and peace; his grip never tires. God's grip heals. There is no way we can wiggle out of his loving grip; therefore, we do not need to panic. His hand of love is always upon us to guide, protect, and direct our paths and to pull back the layers so our brilliance can shine. His love redeems us. So, rest in his presence.

Confession

When storms arise, there is no need for panic because God is my anchor and has a firm grip on my life.

SoulScript

_____

_____

_____

_____

_____

_____

_____

_____

Take a moment to be vulnerable with God (and yourself); write down some things that you have felt panicked about—it could be finances, a loved one, health (mental and/or physical), safety, things going on in our world, or maybe an area where you've felt like a fraud or imposter. God is your provider and here to help you become exactly who he created you to be.

Day 10 – You Are Powerful, Loving, and Have a Well-Balanced Mind

For God did not give us a spirit of timidity (of cowardice, of craven and cringing and fawning fear),
but [He has given us a spirit] of power and of love and of calm and well-balanced
mind and discipline and self-control.
—2 Timothy 1:7 AMPC

If God didn't give it to you, don't take it! Make a choice to believe and receive only what God himself has given you: power, love, calm, a well-balanced mind, discipline, and self-control. Claim each of these as you navigate life. These traits are enhanced by practicing the SHOTS(SS), which are essentially about relationship with God and living with daily discipline.

As I diligently practice specifically the last SHOT, strengthen, I am growing spiritually as an individual and as a member of my community. I am exhibiting a deeper level of calm and self-control. In the past, I had issues during workouts that required the paramedics to be called. I know crazy, right! That was scary. For a while fear prevented me from working out, and my eating habits didn't help. Thankfully, I have seen myself evolve from overindulging in sweets and anything that tastes good to exercising self-discipline in my eating and working out. I have run a couple of races and maintained a consistent Holy Yoga practice; I also started participating in a couple of winter sports, a walking group, and much more. Like choosing courage, living with discipline is a daily choice that fuels my soul and causes me to push myself in ways that make me proud and often inspire others!

Confession

In God's power, I am moving through life with a loving and calm spirit. I have a well-balanced mind and operate with daily discipline and self-control.

SoulScript

_____

_____

_____

_____

_____

_____

_____

List some areas in which you need to exercise more discipline. Choose one of those areas and make a daily plan. Find an accountability partner to help you; don't forget to ask how you can help them too. Iron sharpens iron.

Quote

Create space for your imagination to soar; it is a great source of motivation and power! Use it to believe, grow, and

give birth to your soulfull life!

Question

Is your soulfull dreaming
time scheduled?
If not, what are you waiting for?

Day 11 – Cheerful Words Give Hope

Worry weighs us down; a cheerful word picks us up.
—Proverbs 12:25

Cheerful words come from cheerful thoughts; cheerful thoughts come from what you're hearing. It's not what you heard that matters, it's what you're hear**ing**. The Bible tells us that faith comes from hearing and hearing by the Word of God. Hearing is continual and affects your thoughts, words, beliefs, and actions. If you are feeling worried about anything, make a decision to speak life into your situation and counter those anxious feelings and thoughts with God's Word. Ask the Holy Spirit if there is anything you need to do differently and look for opportunities to encourage those around you with a positive word. Pay attention to what (e.g., music, television, social media) and who you are allowing to speak into your life. If the words they speak or the life they live weighs you down instead of building you up, you might want to reconsider the depth of that relationship.

Confession

I choose to speak encouraging words to myself and others. I strategically place myself in the presence of life-speakers, soul|stirrers, and purpose-pushers! Iron sharpens iron, and I attract what I give.

SoulScript

_____

_____

_____

_____

_____

_____

_____

I know this is your journal, but today is a great day to send a cheerful note of encouragement. Who will you send the message to? What area of life can you encourage him or her in? Take inventory of what you're hearing. Take inventory of your friends. Put a star next to what and who pushes or pulls purpose out of you. Remove yourself from anyone and anything that isn't edifying your soul. Pray for purpose to be revealed and embraced in the lives of your family and friends.

Day 12 – God Is Coming for You—Hold On

Say to those with fearful hearts, "Be strong, do not fear; your God will come, he will come with vengeance; with divine retribution he will come to save you."
—Isaiah 35:4 NIV

God is always in pursuit of you. He is your Savior. The house is on fire again! On two occasions while at my grandmother's house, our house was set on fire in the middle of the night or early morning as we were sound asleep. Someone was out to hurt us and send a message of fear, but God saved us! Each time, my grandmother and I lived to tell about it. God sent neighbors to save us.

It took some time, but I forgave the man who started both fires (we knew him), but he still has to answer to God. For years after the fires, I had a hard time sleeping. I would fall asleep only to wake up off and on throughout the night full of fear, thinking I smelled smoke. During those times, I would have soul|talks about my future; interestingly enough, I am now living in the relational peace I desired and visualized then. God was listening; he heard my soul|desires. I didn't know much about God at the time, but thankfully he knew everything about me. And then, like now, he is in pursuit of me. He keeps drawing, protecting, loving, directing, and providing for me. He has saved me over and over again. God always comes for me. I rest in knowing that he is pursuing, saving, and protecting me.

Confession

Lord, thank you for being my Savior!

SoulScript

_____

_____

_____

_____

_____

_____

_____

_____

What does being "saved" by God look like to you?

Quote

You were created to reign!
Your gifts make room for you. As you
embrace and develop your gifts, doors open
for you to walk into spaces God predestined
for you!

Question

How are you
embracing, nurturing, and
using your gifts?

Day 13 – Belief Changes the Game

As soon as Jesus heard the word that had been spoken, he saith unto the ruler of the
synagogue, Be not afraid, only believe.
—Mark 5:36 KJV

In the Scripture above, the first two words, "As soon," really resonate with me. Over the years, I've learned that as soon as I hear something that doesn't line up with what God says about me, I choose to only believe his word. I don't care if the words spoken come from your mother, if the words are contrary to the word of God, you must immediately remind yourself to only believe in the Word and power of God. Sync your soul with what God says!

In my senior year of high school, I told my guidance counselor that I wanted to go to college. I wanted to be the first in my immediate family to attend and graduate from college. Sure, I hadn't been a strong student and the thought of college didn't come to me until my senior year, but hey, a college degree was what my soul desired. But my counselor promptly told me I was not college material and that my best bet was to find a job in the community. I felt small sitting in his office, somewhat afraid about life and embarrassed that I hadn't been a better student. I believed the words he spoke and acted accordingly! I left his office, went down the hall to the job placement office, got a few referrals, which led to an interview and job offer with a community employer. I worked that job with diligence!

After some time, I began to hear the Word of God more frequently and to learn what God says about me. I chose to believe, embrace, and act on what God said. My soul put a demand on my desire. I enrolled in college, and my community employer helped finance my education (God is so good). While working eight hours a day, being a wife and mother of two, I graduated from a private university magna cum laude. And I did so with very little debt. It took me a minute, but I learned to continually choose to believe what God says about me and the desires of my soul. After graduation, I sat in my corner office and gave God all the praise! The counselor's job was to guide me, but God was and is the ultimate guide. He led me to a job straight out of high school that had amazing benefits (e.g., a 401k plan, tuition and daycare reimbursement) and gave me favor with those in authority over me.

Confession

When I hear words that are not life-bearing whether they are spoken by me or someone else, I immediately cancel out those words with the Word of God. I fear not and choose to only believe what God says about and to me through his Word.

_____

_____

_____

_____

_____

_____

_____

In what area of your life have words been spoken that propel you toward fearful thoughts
or actions? Acknowledge how those words make you feel by writing your feelings down. Now
write down what God says about you and your situation and choose to only believe what God says.
How can you begin to move toward your soul|desires?

Day 14 – You Are Chosen and Have the Right to Choose

But you are not like that, for you are a chosen people. You are royal priests, a holy nation, God's very own possession. As a result, you can show others the goodness of God, for he called you out of the darkness into his wonderful light.
—1 Peter 2:9 NLT

I was born to teenage parents in the early 1970s. I presume that they both heard a lot of unsolicited opinions about the pregnancy and carried their own doubts and shame. I imagine my mother must have been afraid, yet in the face of fear, she somehow understood the assignment and tapped into courage. I know that I would not have had the same courage she had. Understanding your assignment is crucial. It doesn't mean that your life is perfect or without trials, but it means that God is with you in your imperfection and every trial as you complete your assignments. In spite of their age, shortcomings, and everything else, I believe my parents were chosen for me.

Chosen means having been selected as the best or most appropriate. Doesn't it feel good to know that God sees you as the most appropriate, his best, his chosen? The same God who spoke the sun, moon, stars, ocean, and mountains into existence saw fit to add your brilliance to creation. Jesus is the High Priest and as believers and royal priests, we are to reflect the goodness of God in our families, careers, and schools—wherever we go. He has called us out of darkness and into his light. *The chosen ones have a choice.* Don't go back to the dark place(s) in your mind or actions—the place out of which God has already called you! He called you so that he could shine brilliantly through you as you answer the call. You get to choose how you show up and who you show up with and for whom. In spite of how you or I came into this world, God chose us and infused us with brilliance. We all have the freedom to choose—even when it comes to a relationship with God. Choosing is a gift—choose wisely.

Confession

I am chosen by and belong to God. I am showing others the night-and-day difference serving him has made in my life. I'm living in the light now, and my brilliance is shining brightly. I am God's best. I choose people and activities that nurture my soul.

SoulScript

What dark places (e.g., addiction, fear, adultery, abuse, lying, shame, mental torment) have you come out of? Or what dark places do you need to let go of? God is calling; will you answer? How is God's goodness evident in your life? Are you showing and sharing with others the difference God has made in your life?

Quote

How much will do you have?

Annamaria Hernandez

Question

Are you willing
to be uncomfortable for
growth and legacy?

Day 15 – Endorsed by God

*But now, GOD's Message, the God who made you in the first place, Jacob, the One who got you started, Israel: "Don't be afraid, I've redeemed you. I've called your name. You're mine.
When you're in over your head, I'll be there with you. When you're in rough waters, you will not go down. When you're between a rock and a hard place, it won't be a dead end— Because I am GOD, your personal God, The Holy of Israel, your Savior. I paid a huge price for you: all of Egypt, with rich Cush and Seba thrown in! That's how much you mean to me! That's how much I love you! I'd sell off the whole world to get you back, trade the creation just for you.*
—Isaiah 43:1-4

There are some spaces we enter that cause us to feel as if we don't belong. Some of us can even feel out of place with our own family. Sometimes, we may find ourselves in situations that make us feel like we are in over our heads. But rest assured God called you into existence. He created you; he is with you in tough times; he loves you and he wants to be in daily fellowship with you.

Understanding your position is crucial; you are God's masterpiece! If you don't understand your position and who put you there, you will go through life constantly questioning your ability and assignments. God placed his personal stamp of approval on you. He is your personal God. He formed you, and within you, he placed purpose, gifts, and ability. The Scripture above reminds us that though we will have many challenges and scars, each one is proof that we are overcomers through Christ. When it feels like you've hit a roadblock and can no longer move forward, try turning to the right or the left, God will redirect your path. He is with you in the valleys, he redeems you, he loves you—just as you are . . . beautifully broken!

Confession

I have been endorsed by God; he is with me.
There is a seat for me at God's table and at
every table to which he has assigned me.

Soul Script

Today, I want you to write this message to yourself: "I am loved, redeemed, endorsed, and wanted by God. I am his." Meditate on thoughts of belonging to God and being loved, redeemed, endorsed, and wanted by him.

Day 16 – God's Comfort Delights My Soul

In the multitude of my [anxious] thoughts within me, Your comforts cheer and delight my soul!
—Psalm 94:19 AMPC

Your mind can be a cage for fear or the catalyst for soul|full living; you get to choose. We must slow down and take captive every thought that is contrary to the Word of God. Don't let negative thoughts use your mind as a dance floor or playground. When negative thoughts show up, let them know that this is war and they just stepped on a landmine where enemy targets are disabled and destroyed with the Word of God. Your soul will be comforted, grateful, and joyous.

Confession

When anxious thoughts begin to multiply within me, I divide them with the Word of God.

SoulScript

_____

_____

_____

_____

_____

_____

_____

_____

Take a moment to refresh your soul and listen to your favorite worship song. Write the chorus in this portion of the book; you may also want to share the song with a loved one.

Quote

Always believe in the good
your imagination has to offer!
You have the power to imagine
and live the soul full life
you were created for!

Question

What does acting on your
beliefs + soul dreams
look like to you?

Day 17 – God's Presence Comforts and Protects

*Even when I walk through the darkest valley, I will not be afraid, for you are close behind
me. Your rod and your staff protect and comfort me.*
—Psalm 23:4 NLT

Shepherds stay close to their sheep and use a staff to guide them and to lean on for rest. The rod is used to pull sheep out of unfortunate situations and defend them from predators. God is all around you, protecting you from the predator of your soul. God's rod and staff comfort you by being your rest, your guide, and your protection. Even when it looks like you are surrounded by darkness, you are surrounded by God's love, protection, peace, provision, and victory. I am so thankful that our Shepherd is always close to me and those I love. I have wished a time or two though that I could use his rod to deal with predators that have approached my daughters. But God is their Shepherd, not me, right?

Confession

Hallelujah, I am not alone! I will not be overcome with fear. You, God, are my comfort and protection. Your love surrounds me like a flood.

SoulScript

_____

_____

_____

_____

_____

_____

_____

_____

Take some time to meditate on Psalm 23 today. This can be done by reading the psalm and sitting quietly with it, writing the psalm in your journal, or listening to the song or audio Bible.

Day 18 – Storms Demand Faith

When Jesus woke up, he rebuked the wind and said to the waves, "Silence! Be still!"
Suddenly the wind stopped, and there was a great calm. Then he asked them, "Why are
you afraid? Do you still have no faith?"
—Mark 4:39–40 NLT

How do you react in the midst of opposition and fear? It is tempting to lose hope and to be full of fear. Don't shrink back when the winds and waves of life are surrounding you. These are opportunities to evolve and stretch your faith. Notice that when Jesus spoke, the wind suddenly stopped. We too have the power to speak in faith and experience sudden changes in our lives. Speak the word to the wind and waves of life. When you increase your faith, you decrease your fear!

The waves of life are currently coming at my husband and me strongly as we care for one parent who has dementia and another who is experiencing chronic pain. Additionally, a traumatic incident, health issues, loneliness, depression, domestic violence, and anxiety are affecting some of the people we love most in this world. Still, other loved ones are fighting cancer, financial problems, and mental health issues. Of course, like you, we are also navigating "normal" life: marriage, parenting, our own midlife changes, health, careers, and dreams—all while living through a few pandemics! We have a choice to either be pushed to and fro by the winds and waves or to speak to the wind and waves and rest in God's peace, trusting that he has everything under control!

Although some days are harder than others, we choose to focus on the great calm (God's peace) in the midst of the storm. I've heard it said that sometimes God calms the storm, and sometimes he calms you. Part of the peace we carry is that God has given us a vision for our family, and we choose to believe that even when life is "storming," God is orchestrating behind the scenes to bring that vision to pass! That assurance gives us hope for the present and the future. As we exercise faith and speak to the "winds" of life, we have experienced sudden changes in some areas. In other areas we are continuing to hope and believe as we stand on the promises of God. God remains faithful.

Confession

I choose to silence the "winds" of life and increase my faith and calm through my words and time spent in God's presence. I am courageous, and my faith is in God!

Soul Script

_____

_____

_____

_____

_____

_____

_____

_____

What areas are you aware of that you need to rebuke the "winds" and silence the "waves" of life? Write down one or two areas of concern and find Scriptures to stand on— Scriptures that increase your faith and calm in these areas. There comes a time when we or the people we love need additional help balancing all that life throws at us, so don't overlook the gift and healing power of therapy.

Quote

Your choices are leading you toward or away from your soul|assignments. They not only impact you but future generations as well.

Question

What role has fear played when it comes to your choices?

Day 19 – God Doesn't Do Recalls

God's gifts and God's call are under full warranty—never canceled, never rescinded.
—Romans 11:29

Everybody likes an unlimited, bumper-to-bumper warranty covered by the manufacturer. Well, that's exactly what you've been given! No amount of procrastination, excuses, trauma, feelings of inadequacy, or fear can change your soul|assignments. Yes, you need to deal with issues accordingly, but they don't negate your soul|calling—your brilliance. In fact, God will use those very issues to prepare and develop your character. Don't waste time pursuing what you already possess; walk in and pour out your brilliance on others.

Confession

Every gift and call that God gave me is mine and for his glory. He has not, nor will he ever, change his mind about me!

SoulScript

_____

_____

_____

_____

_____

_____

_____

_____

Are you saying yes to God's call and the gifts he's given you? If so, write what your corresponding action looks like. Belief comes alive at the point of action. Talk to God and write down your plan of action.

Day 20 – Give Your Worries to God

Let him have all your worries and cares, for he is always thinking about you and watching
everything that concerns you.
—1 Peter 5:7 TLB

God is always thinking about you! He is standing with his arms open waiting for you to place your worries in his hands. He watches over the word he spoke over you and the assignments he placed in you. Let him have your worries and don't take them back.

Confession

Lord, you are mindful of me, and you perfect the things that concern me. You turn my worries into wonders and my cares into calm.

SoulScript

_____

_____

_____

_____

_____

_____

_____

List everything that is worrying you and take time every day to lay your hand on the list and thank God that he watches, that he cares, and that he is working behind the scenes to straighten it all out. Thank him for the wisdom as to how you are to proceed.

Quote

Finish the race you were born to win.

There is a one-of-a-kind soul|prize with your name on it! Don't get it twisted and compare your race to anyone else's. No one can win your race, and you can't win anyone else's. If you attempt to run someone else's race, you are guaranteed to lose . . . twice!

Question

Are you doubting God
by comparing
your God-given brilliance
to someone else's?

Day 21 – God Is Working on Your Behalf

And we know that in all things God works for the good of those who love him, who have been called according to his purpose.
—Romans 8:28 NIV

You're reading this devotional, so I believe you love God. He created and predestined you, so I know he's called you to his purpose. In **all** things, God is working for your good. If you didn't know that, now you know! *All* means **all**, so this includes the things that other people brought upon you as well as the things you've brought upon yourself. If it isn't all good yet, it isn't all done yet!

Thank God that he has a plan and purpose for your life; he is turning things around for your good so his Word can come to pass. Even the seemingly messy parts of your story—God wants to use those for good too. The ugly parts of your story will make your comeback greater, build character, bless others, and bring him glory. The world sees God through you; his reputation is on the line, and he will defend his great name. Align yourself with his purpose and get ready for the good!

Confession

I am called to God's purpose. He is completing a good work in me, building perseverance while working all things for my good and his glory!

SoulScript

_____

_____

_____

_____

_____

_____

_____

_____

Take a praise break! The things you see and don't see—he's working it all out for your good, so his purpose can come to fruition. Won't he do it!!

Day 22 – Hope and Cheer Are Salve for the Soul

Lord, when doubts fill my mind, when my heart is in turmoil, quiet me and give me
renewed hope and cheer.
—Psalm 94:19 TLB

Look for joy in adversity! Joy is a fruit of the Spirit, an inner gladness that you can fill up on, bubble over with, and pour out in spite of challenges. The enemy of your soul will forever and always attempt to serve you a platter of fear and doubt. Even when it seems that he's won, claim courage, strength, and victory as you increase your joy with the Word of God.

When COVID-19 hit the United States, fear and doubt tried to take me out. Yes, I feared that someone I love or I would contract COVID-19, but I also feared because my husband's income was our only income. Initially, his profession came to a screeching halt, so my heart was in turmoil. I had to remind myself that when my mind starts tripping, I have direct access to the reset button! Part of my reset is prayer, worship and, of course, the SHOTS(SS)! During our time of being home, our family of six was given a pause button to connect more deeply, heal, play, and worship together. God renewed our hope and cheer in him and each other as a family! We found joy, peace, and healing in the thick of chaos. And somehow in the midst of our calling the SHOTS(SS), God also gave us plenty for ourselves and plenty to give away.

Confession

The joy of the Lord is my strength!

Soul Script

_____

_____

_____

_____

_____

_____

_____

_____

Are you operating in the fruit of the Spirit? Take some time to meditate on Galatians 5:22–23; talk to the Holy Spirit and ask him to help you operate in the fruit of the Spirit at a higher level. Invite him to help in every aspect of your life. Write down what you believe he's speaking to you.

Quote

You've got what it takes to finish but first, you have to start! You are God's brilliant idea, a once-in-a-lifetime occurrence, with a once-in-a-lifetime opportunity to *do what your soul was created for!*

Question

What is your soul committed to finishing or starting?

Day 23 – A Soul|full Duo

They keep you safe on your way, and your feet will not stumble. You can go to bed without fear; you will lie down and sleep soundly.
—Proverbs 3:23–24 NLT

Who does the word *they* refer to in the Scripture above? If you read the two verses that precede our passage, you will see that the answer is discernment and common sense or sound judgment. As believers, we should have godly discernment and common sense. This power-packed duo will allow you to walk safely and confidently because the path has been cleared for you, and you can see clearly. Common sense and discernment are imperative; you need them in every aspect of life. We should always be praying to receive this duo for ourselves, loved ones, and leaders. In addition to providing a safe and clear path, discernment and common sense refresh your soul, allowing you to go to sleep in peace and have sweet rest! Can I get an amen for sweet rest? If you're having issues sleeping, try listening to some worship music or confessions at bedtime.

Confession

I operate with godly discernment, common sense, and sound judgment that cause me not to stumble. Glory to God, I sleep peacefully and soundly. Even as I sleep, the Holy Spirit is filling my soul with peace, wisdom, direction, and joy!

SoulScript

_____

_____

_____

_____

_____

_____

_____

_____

_____

List the areas in which you or a loved one needs to exercise godly discernment, common sense, and sound judgment. Begin to thank God for providing all that is needed!

Day 24 – Let's Get It

Then he continued, "Be strong and courageous and get to work. Don't be frightened by the size of the task, for the Lord my God is with you; he will not forsake you. He will see to it that everything is finished correctly.
—1 Chronicles 28:20 TLB

We've read "be strong and courageous" multiple times in the Bible, and hopefully, can agree that it is a command our souls are capable of! I love this verse because of the words, "get to work!" Can I get a handclap for doing the work? Y'all, those words spoke to me: *"Tiffane, do the work God called you to do!"* The work I do now will outlive me and become my legacy. Regardless of what is or isn't going on around me, I am responsible for doing what God called me to do. Ecclesiastes 11:4, which I cited in the Introduction, makes it clear that we are not to wait for conditions to be perfect, or we won't accomplish anything!

What we believe will become apparent by the words we speak and most certainly by our actions. God has gifted you to do what he created you for, but you can't do it standing still—you have to move! My favorite childhood fairy tales and the popular R&B music of the '80s and '90s had me thinking that marriage was all fun and play or at least, that was my interpretation. In reality, having a healthy marriage takes work (i.e., *discipline* —yep there's that word again), and with the work comes freedom, healing, and vulnerability that lead to fun and play! For my husband and me, when truth was exposed, we realized that just like anything else worth having, our marriage would require work, sacrifice, forgiveness, and intentionality. Part of being intentional for us means having a blueprint guided by God, and our commitment to do the work daily has brought us a mighty long way.

When you do the work in any of your relationships, it makes fun and playing attainable and gives you an unparalleled level of love and intimacy. You can read more about our marriage journey on my blog at www.simplytchic.com.

Confession

I am strong, courageous, and equipped to do the work my soul was created for!

Soul Script

_____

_____

_____

_____

_____

_____

_____

What work have you been called to do? Pray over your calling; consider and write what practical moves you can implement right now to begin the work. The work could be prayer for yourself or for your relationships, health, business, finances, or another area. Don't be discouraged by the size of the task; be encouraged that you have what it takes to complete the assignment.

Quote

Life Talk

no in-between talk

Death Talk

Are you speaking life
to yourself and others? How do
you acknowledge those that
speak life to your soul?

Day 25 – Problems Don't Stop God's Provision

He does not fear bad news, nor live in dread of what may happen. For he is settled in his
mind that Jehovah will take care of him.
—Psalm 112:7 TLB

With fear-talk all around us, we can still choose faith-talk. Faith-talk fuels the soul and directs our confidence and trust to the one who created us. At the time of this writing, we are in the midst of a few pandemics: Coronavirus disease, polarization of political parties like never before, and an outcry for racial justice and systemic change. Additionally, inflation continues to increase, and yet, our God is still on the throne! Neither our personal problems nor the world's problems are a surprise to God. Pandemic does not stop purpose, and it certainly does not stop God's provision!

Confession

Jehovah-Shalom, you are my peace.
Jehovah-Jireh, you are my provider.
Jehovah-Rapha, you are my healer.

Soul Script

Day 26 – Wholehearted Dedication + Action Gets Results

Having started the ball rolling so enthusiastically, you should carry this project through to completion just as gladly, giving whatever you can out of whatever you have. Let your enthusiastic idea at the start be equalled by your realistic action now.
—2 Corinthians 8:11 TLB

Oftentimes, we start goals, assignments, devotions, exercise plans, relationships, and healthy eating with great enthusiasm but lose energy when things become mundane or challenging. If it is a God-assignment, pray for soul|sourced wisdom, creativity, and energy to keep going. If you don't quit, you will learn so much, and eventually you will win.

This devotional was started with enthusiasm; seeing it through has been challenging as this is my first time working on a project like this, and life doesn't stop because I am working on a devotional. If anything, my life has become more intense and demanded more of me in recent months! But through the process, I am becoming more of who I was created to be, and I refuse to quit until I finish! Wholehearted commitment isn't easy, but when we give what we can from what we have, we can see things to completion and enjoy soul|rest! You've made it this far; keep going. Your soul|sourced zeal fueled with action will get you to completion. Don't forget to celebrate the small victories along the way.

Confession

I finish what I start, and I finish well.

SoulScript

_____

_____

_____

_____

_____

_____

_____

_____

_____

Take a moment to write down how far you've come.

Quote

A soul|full life is developed over time, not overnight. Remember to give yourself grace **and extend it to others too!**

Question

How are you
embracing and extending
grace to yourself and others?

Day 27 – New Things Can Be Very Exciting

For I'm going to do a brand-new thing. See, I have already begun! Don't you see it? I will make a road through the wilderness of the world for my people to go home, and create rivers for them in the desert!
—Isaiah 43:19 TLB

The wonderful thing about serving God is that he is always up to something good, something new; that's just who he is! Believe that he is doing a good, new thing for you and your family, relationships, health, career, education, and life. Get excited!

I don't know what's next, but I trust God! I am looking forward to growing old gracefully and reflecting on how God brought new life to things I thought were dying or dead, aren't you?

Confession

God has begun a good work in me. He is doing a new thing, and I'm here for all of it!

SoulScript

_____

_____

_____

_____

_____

_____

_____

Write down the areas of your life in which you need God to do a new thing. Start talking and acting like it is so. Have you noticed any changes in your mind and behaviors since starting this devotional? Write them down. Give God praise for what he has done, what he is doing, and what is to come! Please email me (simplytchic@gmail.com) a message or a video recording of how this experience has blessed you, so I can rejoice with you. I'll be waiting!

Day 28 – Victory Belongs to You

Yet amid all these things we are more than conquerors and gain a surpassing victory
through Him Who loved us.
—Romans 8:37 AMPC

The fact that you are living tells me that you have overcome some hard things, and I am sure you have the scars to prove it. Ask God to show you who he wants you to share your "scar" story with. You are more than a conqueror. Don't accept defeat; you may have to change your strategy, but overwhelming victory is in your future! God loves you.

Confession

I am more than a conqueror, and I expect and experience overwhelming victory!

SoulScript

_____

_____

_____

_____

_____

_____

_____

Take some time to imagine and write down what overwhelming victory looks like to you. What does it feel like, what are you wearing, who is there with you? In addition to the Lord, who do you need to thank for encouraging and standing with you through the process? Finally, who are you going to remind that they too are more than a conqueror?

Quote

Keep moving forward
on your journey to a fearless, soul|full life!
Your wins and legacy aren't just for you! Keep
taking SHOTS(SS) and don't you dare keep
them to yourself!

Question

Do you schedule time to *celebrate your wins?*

Day 29 – Your Tongue Has Power

Words kill, words give life; they're either poison or fruit—you choose.
—Proverbs 18:21

Yo, choose fruit—it's much sweeter, and it won't kill you! There is so much power in your tongue. Use your power for good.

Once upon a time, my marriage was struggling—big time! It was easy to speak about the problems because they were staring me in the face. Then one day, Proverbs 18:21 dropped in my spirit, and I felt led to speak and pray for my marriage, my husband, and myself in a way that was strictly edifying! During my quiet time with the Lord, I felt led to read 1 Corinthians 13 each day and put my name in the place of the word *love* and to extend to my husband the same grace and love I would extend to a sister or brother in Christ in moments when loving was difficult. This meant praying for him, loving him, and speaking life to him. I put pictures of us in every room in our house (bathroom included), and every time I walked by a picture, I spoke a life-giving word! We created marriage confessions and spoke them aloud and in our minds whenever needed! As we began to speak life to each other and our marriage, our actions and thoughts began to line up with what we were speaking. Gradually, the manifestation of those words became the fruit of what can be seen today in our twenty-ninth year of marriage!

To this day I continue to protect my marriage with my words. Recently, I felt overwhelmed by all that is going on, and my husband wrapped his arms around me and encouraged me with God's Word by praying and speaking life over me and the situations that were overwhelming me. I was filled with so much peace and gratitude. I am so glad we didn't throw in the towel 20 years earlier as we were becoming.

Confession

I speak life-giving, soul|filling words even in the face of trials.

SoulScript

_____

_____

_____

_____

_____

_____

_____

Look at yourself in a mirror (if you can) and repeat aloud a quote or confession from this devotional that you need right now! Write the quote or confession down in your journal. Create a voice memo on your phone and record yourself speaking life to yourself; listen to it daily! Record one for a friend and send it to them!

Day 30 – Are You Fighting the Right Opponent?

And that about wraps it up. God is strong, and he wants you strong. So take everything the Master has set out for you, well-made weapons of the best materials. And put them to use so you will be able to stand up to everything the Devil throws your way. This is no weekend war that we'll walk away from and forget about in a couple of hours. This is for keeps, a life-or-death fight to the finish against the Devil and all his angels.
—Ephesians 6:10–12

Don't believe the hype! It's not your father, mother, sister, brother, friend, husband, wife, or children you are warring with. It is so easy to become upset and harbor unforgiveness with family, friends, coworkers, or neighbors—it's not worth it. The enemy of your soul would love to keep you distracted from soul|full living with anything, including fighting the very people who are supposed to be on your team. Keep your armor up. Don't waste your weapons in the carnal realm. The battle is ultimately for the soul. Fight to the finish with the weapons God has for you. This is not a drill. If you sit on the sidelines, you and/or someone you love risks being wounded by enemy fire!

Confession

My strength comes from the Lord's mighty power! My battles are not against flesh and blood but against the principalities and powers of the unseen world. I keep my God-given armor on and buffed, so I can stand against the schemes of the enemy.

Soul Script

A real soldier familiarizes herself or himself with their weapons before the battle. Create some time to read Ephesians 6:11–20. Buff your armor and take your SHOTS(SS)!

148

Quote

You have been presented with a choice: live from your soul or dim your God-given brilliance and live as an imposter—with regret. I pray you choose the former!

Question

In what ways can you
unleash your brilliance today?

Day 31 – Expect More

Now glory be to God, who by his mighty power at work within us is able to do far more than we would ever dare to ask or even dream of—infinitely beyond our highest prayers, desires, thoughts, or hopes.
—Ephesians 3:20 TLB

If I were to tell you to think of a specific dollar amount that I could bless you with, how much would you ask for? The amount might vary based on what you believe I could afford, your perceived need, or what you feel you deserve from me. If you knew I was a billionaire, would your ask be bigger? This Scripture tells us that God can do far more than we can dream. The Scripture challenges us to take the limits off God, our imaginations, prayers, and dreams! The how isn't for us to figure out. I believe that when we dare to ask, dream, and move forward in faith, the how is revealed by God.

It doesn't matter what has happened or what is going on in your life, know that God is able to do more than you can ask or dream when you are aligned with his will. He can do more in and through you, more in your relationships, and more in your finances and health. Fear is a waste and abuse of your imagination; remember to use your imagination for infinite dreams. Dream, think, hope, and pray for what your soul really desires. I can't wait to see what God has in store for you and me!

Confession

Lord, your mighty power is at work in my life, and I am expecting you to show up and show completely out like only you can do!

Soul|Script

_____

_____

_____

_____

_____

_____

_____

_____

Take some time to sit still in God's presence, just you and your soul|sourced dreams. If fear, resources, and other people's opinions weren't an issue, what would you dare to dream? What is your ask of God? Imagine and write down your ask; believe and pray over it.

The Soul|Full Confession

Our words have power. We can see this in Genesis when God spoke the world into existence and throughout the Bible. In the process of becoming our most brilliant selves, we must continually renew our minds and speak things into existence. This "Soul|Confession" can be used as a daily affirmation or simply read as a reminder when needed as part of your transformation:

I am God's brilliant idea—strong and courageous! He placed in me everything I need to live soul|fully. I am nurturing my soul with God's Word and my words and actions. I operate in power, love, and a sound mind. I will not let fear get in the way of manifesting my brilliance. I embrace a lifestyle of faith, discipline, serving, and maximizing time by seeking God for clear vision. I choose to speak life into every situation, recognizing that my words have power. When I fall, I get up, adjust, and keep moving toward the victory that awaits my soul. I surround myself with soul|motivators and together, we navigate the valleys and triumphs of life.
I expect to win because I was born to win. I live to bring glory to God while completing the mission of my soul. I shine brilliantly, encourage others to do the same, and leave a soul|full legacy!

Soul|Full Permission Slip

God's already given you permission to be great; so take it. Give notice to fear and stop asking for permission to be brilliant. Your right to have more fearless moments, to be brilliant is inherent—a gift given to you before you were born. Use this "permission slip" as a reminder to give yourself permission to take action toward the courageous moves you want to make. The time to be courageous is now.

What will you give yourself permission to do/say/be or no longer do/say/be? How does taking your power back and giving yourself permission to be great make you feel? Who will support you on your journey to soul|full brilliance?

I give myself fearless permission to:

soul|full permission

A Word to the Reader

Hey Soul|Friends,

Thank you so much for sharing this journey with me! I would love to hear from you! If I could, I would invite you to sit under my pergola so we could share a cup of tea and some soul|baring conversation; we would have a soul|full time. Since we can't do that, I welcome an email from you sharing prayer requests and testimonies, or you can let me know how this devotional has encouraged you or someone you love to live soul|fully.

Email me if you'd like to share your Soul|full Permission Slip with me or if you'd like to receive a digital copy of the Permission Slip. To share your permission slip, you can simply email it to me or post it on Instagram and tag me (@simplytchic) if that's more your speed. Please note that I will not share your permission slip or testimony without your permission.

Another way we can connect is through my website where you can see what I'm up to, maybe attend a soul|full conversation, and subscribe to my very occasional newsletter!

Sending love, soul|sourced energy, and Tiff hugs . . .

Email: simplytchic@gmail.com
Website: www.simplytchic.com

Acknowledgments: Soul|Full Gratitude

Soul|friend, I do not take the gift of your purchase and reading this devotional lightly! I hope you are blessed and motivated to live more from your soul after engaging with this devotional.

To my lover for life, Roger, thank you for being my copilot, extra set of eyes, sounding board, and support in all the good that I do! If anyone appreciates the creativity of my hands or words, they should know that you have been involved behind the scenes in some way.

GGs, you are four of the reasons I choose courage. My soul has and always will love you and pray for you to live soul|fully. Always remember to tap into your GPS (God Positioning System) for direction. Fuel your soul with God and goodness and when you think you don't know the way, trust that your soul does!

To my Mom, Terry, who at the tender age of 16 literally chose to protect and push out God's brilliant idea (me). Without you, without your courage, there is no me!

To my sister by choice, Dawn, thank you for returning from sabbatical and going to the deep end with me.

To my cousin, Victor, thank you for encouraging and supporting everything I do. It's a blessing to know that you are always rooting for me.

To my purpose-pushers and soul|motivators, thank you for praying, pushing, and pulling purpose out of me. Special thanks to L.M., F.B., N.F., and M.T.

To my maternal and paternal grandmothers, Catherine and Jeanne, thank you for all that you imparted to me before you left and for your ongoing presence in my life. Your love continues to fuel my soul.

To the one who holds my soul, you have been many things to me: Father, friend, peace, provider, protector, victory, courage, savior, and more! Thank you for infusing me with the desire and ability to live soul|fully while bringing you glory through service to others. Thank you for putting your stamp of approval on me. I am eternally grateful for your love as it is always in pursuit of me!

With soul|full gratitude,
Tiffane

Made in the USA
Monee, IL
15 March 2023